THE OCEAN BIOME

Colin Grady

Enslow Publishing
101 W. 23rd Street
Suite 240
New York, NY 10011
USA

enslow.com

WORDS TO KNOW

climate—The weather conditions in a place over a period of years.

community—A group of living things that share the same area.

currents—The flow or stream of water.

erupt—To violently send out steam and lava.

gravel—Small loose pieces of rock.

mammals—Warm-blooded animals with backbones.

mineral—Solid matter that comes from the earth.

oceanographers—Scientists who study the oceans and the living things in them.

plains—Large, flat, open areas of land that have no trees.

pollution—Anything that makes a place dirty, especially waste.

submarines—Boats that are made to work underwater.

CONTENTS

The ocean is the world's largest biome.

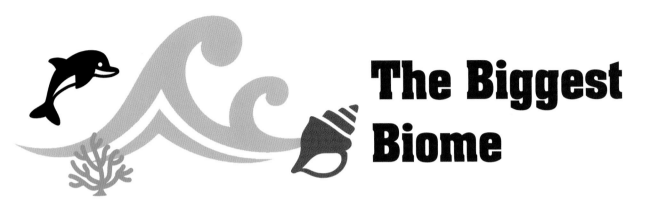

The Biggest Biome

A biome is a community of plants and animals that live together in a certain place and climate. There are different types of biomes, such as grasslands and deserts. The ocean is another kind of biome.

The ocean biome is the largest biome on earth. It covers more than 70 percent of the earth's surface. The Pacific,

Atlantic, Arctic, Indian, and Southern Oceans make up the ocean biome.

The Rich Sea

The ocean biome gives us food, energy, and minerals. We eat many of the plants and animals living in the ocean. Energy comes from oil and natural gas found in

Our Newest Ocean

For a long time there were just four main oceans: the Atlantic, Pacific, Indian, and Arctic. Around the year 2000, though, most countries (including the United States) began to recognize a fifth ocean area, the Southern Ocean. It is located at the most southern part of the earth, and it is sometimes called the Antarctic Ocean.

The Biggest Biome

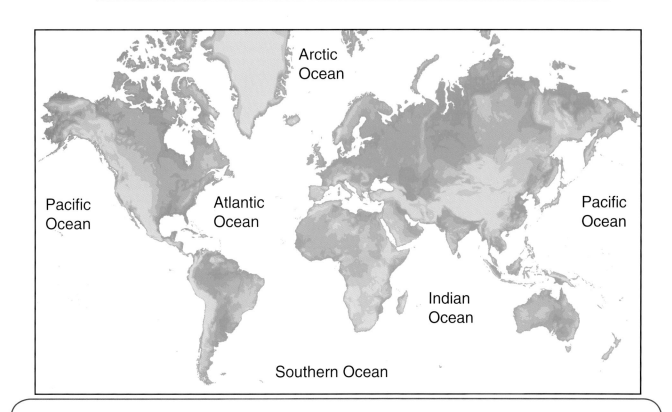

Most of the water on earth is found in the oceans. Without the oceans, there would be no life on earth.

the ocean floor. Minerals, sand, and gravel are taken from the bottom of the oceans and are used to make building materials.

The oceans give us much of the food we eat. These fishermen are pulling up nets of salmon.

Life in the Ocean

The ocean floor is a very interesting place! In fact, it has a lot of the same things that we have on land except they are underwater. There are huge mountain ranges in the ocean, and many rise thousands of feet high. You can also find deep valleys and wide plains on the ocean floor. There are even underwater volcanoes! They can erupt just like the ones on land.

Life in the Ocean

The three groups of ocean life are the plankton, the nekton, and the benthos. Plankton are plantlike creatures and animals that are small and weak. They drift with ocean currents because they are not strong enough to swim. Nekton are animals that swim freely in the ocean. Fish, squid, and ocean mammals, such as dolphins, are nekton.

An underwater volcano gives off smoke.

Some of the creatures that live in the deep ocean, such as this anglerfish, are very unusual. Some do not have eyes, and others glow in the dark.

Benthos are sea creatures that live on or near the ocean floor. These include starfish, mussels, and sea anemones.

Many Kinds of Life

Ocean plants and animals grow to many different sizes. Some, such as plankton, are so small they cannot be seen without microscopes. Larger animals, such as the blue

Many plants live on the ocean floor.

whale, can be as long as 100 feet (30 meters). Plants can live up to 330 feet (100 meters) below the surface of the water. The sunlight that plants need to live does not reach below that point.

Mammals in the Ocean

There are many mammals that live in the water, but they all still need to breathe air. Some ocean animals need to come up for air every twenty seconds. Other mammals, like certain whales, can hold their breath for over an hour.

Dolphins live and travel in groups called pods.

Moving Water

Have you ever wondered what causes the waves in the ocean? They are mostly caused by wind. Some of the wind's energy is moved to the water. The faster and stronger the wind is, the bigger the waves are. In the waves, water moves up and down, not forward. When it gets near the shore, the wave moves forward and crashes on the beach.

Strong winds may cause huge waves to form in the ocean.

Giant Waves

Tsunamis (su-NAH-meehz) are giant waves that are made by underwater earthquakes. They can travel as fast as 600 miles (966 kilometers) per hour and can be 100 feet (30 meters) high. Tsunamis can be very dangerous if they reach land.

Ocean Tides

Tides are the rise and fall of the water's level. The tides are caused by the pull of the moon and sun. Waters in the ocean usually rise for about six hours and then go down for about six hours. This is what causes low tide and high tide when you are at the beach.

Learning About the Ocean

There is a lot to learn about the ocean. In fact, since the ocean is so huge, most of it has never been explored. Oceanographers are scientists who study the ocean. They help us continue to learn about the ocean. In 1977, oceanographers found places in the deep ocean that were home to entire communities of plants and animals. The scientists never knew that these places were there.

17

An oceanographer on a research ship works with a piece of equipment that will help him learn more about the ocean.

Spilling Into Our Oceans

Sometimes accidents happen in the ocean that cause large amounts of oil to be spilled into the water. One recent spill happened in the Gulf of Mexico in 2010. This is dangerous for ocean life, as well as for humans.

Oceanographers use ships up to three hundred feet long to explore the ocean. They also have submarines that can take them deep into the ocean. Studying the ocean helps scientists understand the earth's weather and life in the sea.

Caring for the Ocean

Trash and junk are often dumped into the ocean. This is called pollution. People have polluted the oceans for many years. We need to keep our ocean biome free of pollution so it continues to provide us with the things we need.

This pelican is covered with oil after an explosion spilled tons of oil into the ocean in 2010.

ACTIVITY
FISH VERSUS MAMMAL

In this book, you learned that nekton are all animals that swim freely in the ocean. This includes fish and mammals. Even though they are all part of this one group, fish and mammals are different in many ways.

1. Choose one kind of fish and one kind of mammal (for example, a flounder and a whale). You can research online to find your animals.

2. On a blank piece of paper, draw the overlapping circles seen on page 23.

3. Label one circle with your fish and the other with your mammal. What do your two animals have in common? Again, check for information online to find out more about the animals.

4. Write down what is similar in the area in the middle. How are they different? Write down differences in the parts of the two circles that don't overlap. You may want to think about whether they have hair, breathe water or air, lay eggs, have fins, and so on.

5. Did you find more similiarities or differences?

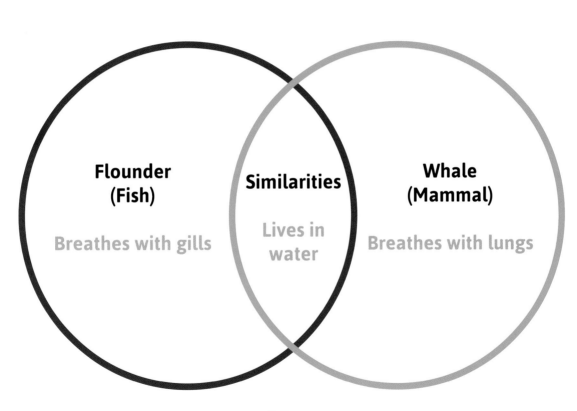

**Flounder
(Fish)**

Breathes with gills

Similarities

Lives in water

**Whale
(Mammal)**

Breathes with lungs

LEARN MORE

Books

Coss, Lauren. *Life in Oceans*. North Mankato, MN: Child's World, 2014.

Duke, Shirley. *Seasons of the Ocean Biome*. Vero Beach, FL: Rourke, 2014.

Johnson, Robin. *Oceans Inside Out*. New York: Crabtree, 2014.

Reynolds, Toby, and Paul Calver. *Ocean Life*. Hauppauge, NY: Barron's, 2015.

Websites

Kids Do Ecology
kids.nceas.ucsb.edu/biomes/marine.html
Photos, facts, and links to information about the oceans.

National Geographic Kids
kids.nationalgeographic.com/explore/ocean-portal/#
Learn more about oceans through games, activities, and videos.

INDEX

Published in 2017 by Enslow Publishing, LLC.
101 W. 23rd Street, Suite 240, New York, NY 10011

Copyright © 2017 by Enslow Publishing, LLC

Library of Congress Cataloging-in-Publication Data

Names: Grady, Colin.
Title: The ocean biome / Colin Grady.
Description: New York, NY : Enslow Publishing, 2017. | "2017 | Series: Zoom in on biomes | Audience: Ages 7+ | Audience: Grades K to 3. | Includes bibliographical references and index.
Identifiers: LCCN 2015048571| ISBN 9780766077904 (library bound) | ISBN 9780766077850 (pbk.) | ISBN 9780766077881 (6-pack)
Subjects: LCSH: Marine ecology--Juvenile literature. | Marine animals--Juvenile literature.
Classification: LCC QH541.5.S3 G7175 2017 | DDC 577.7--dc23
LC record available at http://lccn.loc.gov/2015048571

Printed in Malaysia

Photo Credits: Cover, p. 1 muratart/Shutterstock.com; throughout book, ly86/DigitalVision Vectors/Getty Images (wave graphics); lushik/DigitalVision Vectors/Getty Images (beach and sea life icons); p. 4 ForwardOne/iStock/Thinkstock; p. 7 Designua/Shutterstock.com; p. 8 Rich Reid/National Geographic/Getty Images; p. 10 B. Murton/Southampton Oceanography Centre /Science Source; p. 11 bierchen/Shutterstock.com; p. 12 Kichigin/Shutterstock.com; p. 13 Ruth Petzold/Moment/Getty Images; p. 15 Craig Aurness/Fuse/Thinkstock; p. 18 Dante Fenolio/ Science Source/Getty Images; p. 20 © AP Images; p. 21 Rich Carey/Shutterstock.com.